Bad Company

A Play

Simon Bent

A Samuel French Acting Edition

SAMUELFRENCH-LONDON.CO.UK
SAMUELFRENCH.COM

Copyright © 1994 by Simon Bent
All Rights Reserved

BAD COMPANY is fully protected under the copyright laws of the British Commonwealth, including Canada, the United States of America, and all other countries of the Copyright Union. All rights, including professional and amateur stage productions, recitation, lecturing, public reading, motion picture, radio broadcasting, television and the rights of translation into foreign languages are strictly reserved.

ISBN 978-0-573-01723-0

www.samuelfrench-london.co.uk

www.samuelfrench.com

FOR AMATEUR PRODUCTION ENQUIRIES

UNITED KINGDOM AND WORLD EXCLUDING NORTH AMERICA

plays@SamuelFrench-London.co.uk

020 7255 4302/01

Each title is subject to availability from Samuel French,

depending upon country of performance.

CAUTION: Professional and amateur producers are hereby warned that *BAD COMPANY* is subject to a licensing fee. Publication of this play does not imply availability for performance. Both amateurs and professionals considering a production are strongly advised to apply to the appropriate agent before starting rehearsals, advertising, or booking a theatre. A licensing fee must be paid whether the title is presented for charity or gain and whether or not admission is charged.

The professional rights in this play are controlled by The Agency Ltd, 24 Pottery Lane, Holland Park, London W11 4LZ.

No one shall make any changes in this title for the purpose of production. No part of this book may be reproduced, stored in a retrieval system, or transmitted in any form, by any means, now known or yet to be invented, including mechanical, electronic, photocopying, recording, videotaping, or otherwise, without the prior written permission of the publisher. No one shall upload this title, or part of this title, to any social media websites.

The right of Simon Bent to be identified as author of this work has been asserted by him in accordance with Section 77 of the Copyright, Designs and Patents Act 1988

BAD COMPANY

First performed on 8th February, 1994, at the Bush Theatre, London, with the following cast:

Billy Hayes	Paul Wyett
Paul Turner	Kemal Sylvester
Shirley	Nicola Sanderson
Steven	Nicolas Tennant
Mary	Suzanne Hitchmough
Nicky Tredwell	Gary Sefton
Shirt	Mark Petrie
Ian Smith	Stuart Laing

Directed by Paul Miller
Design by Jane Barwell
Lighting design by Sacha Brooks

CHARACTERS

Billy Hayes
Paul Turner
Shirley
Steven   } all in their early twenties
Mary
Nicky Tredwell
Shirt
Ian Smith

The play takes place in a northern seaside resort (Scarborough)

Time: the present during the summer

Setting
The set should be as minimal and impressionistic as possible, to allow flow from scene to scene. Also atmospheric and evocative of a seaside town during the summer. Only that which is absolutely necessary should be used to represent each setting. Scene changes should be fast and snappy, helping to drive forward the action of the play.

Lighting
The lighting should be uncomplicated and simply reflect the time and place of each scene. However, the Night Club state must catch the atmosphere as much as is possible, without drowning the actors and with the ability to switch quickly to the Gents' toilet.

Sound
Sound effects should only be used where stated in the text. Any music used should be contemporary and drawn from the pop charts. Music should be used sparingly, to add splashes of colour. However, during the Night Club scene continuous background music will be necessary; it should be maintained at an audible level but not loud enough to drown the actors. When Mary dances with Paul the volume can be increased.

Interval
If necessary an interval can be placed between Scene 15 and Scene 16.

Author's Note

I have requested that the expression "all right" be spelled as "alright" throughout my play. I have used this as a colloquialism, meaning "I'm OK" as opposed to "it's all right".

There is minimal punctation in the play as I wanted any such punctuation to act as a guideline to the tempo of the piece and not to interrupt the flow of the play. The dialogue should come off the page as spoken, not written, English. I wanted actors to find their own breath within the lines.

Simon Bent

BAD COMPANY

Scene 1

The beach

Paul and Billy are playing football. Paul, stripped to the waist and barefoot, picks up the ball and bounces it like a basketball

Billy You can't do that.
Paul See that girl.
Billy It's handball.
Paul She's giving us the eye.
Billy Penalty!
Paul She is.

Billy sits

Billy Three and in or I'm not playing.
Paul She's still looking.
Billy I'm gonna get a mountain bike. (*He examines his feet*)
Paul She can't take her eyes off me.
Billy Oh yeah?

Paul looks out to sea

Paul Just smell it will you.
Billy These shoes are killing me.
Paul Go on.
Billy My feet hurt.
Paul Go on.
Billy I think they're swollen.
Paul Take your shoes off.
Billy I don't want to.
Paul Stop complaining then.

Billy Alright. (*He takes his shoes off*)
Paul Look at it. See that rock over there? I had Lee Shipley behind that rock.
Billy Oh aye.
Paul I bloody did.
Billy They are, they're swollen.
Paul She was out of her brain on shoe polish.
Billy You bloody didn't.
Paul You don't believe anyone's ever done it, not even your mam and dad.
Billy Look at them.
Paul Particularly your mam and dad.
Billy I've always had bad feet.
Paul Not anyone's mam and dad. Look at it, that's all I come back for.
Billy You've eaten all the chocolate.
Paul Throw us me T-shirt.

Billy does so. He picks up a postcard

Billy (*reading*) Dear Paul——
Paul Don't read that.
Billy Dear Paul——
Paul Come on.
Billy Dear Paul——
Paul Billy!

They tussle for the card. Paul gets it. Billy snatches it back

Billy (*reading*) Dear Paul—sorry I missed you—hope you had a good journey—might be up in your neck of the woods next week—maybe see you—please write soon—love, J—kiss—kiss.

Paul snatches the card back

   Don't think much of the picture.
Paul What's wrong with it?
Billy I could do better than that.
Paul You wouldn't know which end of the brush to use.
Billy Did you fuck her in London?
Paul Chuck us the ball walnut-brain.

Scene 2

Billy It's punctured.
Paul G'is it here.

Billy throws the ball

No it isn't. Come on.
Billy Alright. Three and in, you're in. (*He shoots at the goal*)

Paul saves it

Shit!

Paul plays basketball

That's handball. Paul!

Paul dribbles round Billy

I'm going.
Paul She's still looking.

Scene 2

Shirley and Steven

Shirley I don't want to.
Steven Why not?
Shirley Because I don't.
Steven Please Shirley.
Shirley I've told you.
Steven Shirley.
Shirley Grow up will you.
Steven Come on, it won't take long.
Shirley I know.
Steven Just the once it happened, one time that's all and you said it didn't matter.
Shirley Well it wasn't worth crying about was it. Any girl so much as looks at you for longer than half a second and you have to change your underwear.

Steven It's only you Shirley, only you do this to me.
Shirley No.
Steven I love you.
Shirley Don't be silly.
Steven But I do.
Shirley You're working yourself up Steven. Mary's waiting for me.
Steven Stuff Mary, I can't go back to work feeling like this.
Shirley You've had a bag of chips.
Steven Why are you doing this to me?
Shirley I'm not doing anything to you. Look, I've got to go.
Steven Shirley!

SCENE 3

The beach

Billy You wouldn't just leave.
Paul No.
Billy You would.
Paul I've only just got back.
Billy Yeah.
Paul I'm not going anywhere I promise.
Billy If you do you'll take me won't you.
Paul I might.
Billy You wouldn't just leave.
Paul No.
Billy Here I've got a mate knows someone lives in London, Alison something.
Paul Oh yeah, I know her.
Billy Short blonde hair from Burniston got married to a bloke down there.
Paul It's a big place Billy. Look at it.
Billy It's alright.
Paul Is it.
Billy What's wrong with it.
Paul I haven't got any money.
Billy I've got money.
Paul I don't want your money.
Billy Alright.

Scene 4

Paul Look at her.
Billy She's alright.
Paul Can I come and stay at your place.
Billy Yeah—why.
Paul Just forget it.
Billy Why.
Paul Give over will you.
Billy But I've only got one bed.
Paul OK—we'll toss for it. Tails it's mine.

Billy throws a coin

Billy Bollocks. Why can't you stay at home.
Paul I can. Look at that will you a cargo ship coming into the harbour.
Billy It's from Norway.
Paul How do you know.
Billy By the colours.

SCENE 4

Café on the edge of the beach

Mary is waiting

Shirley enters

Mary Where's Steven.
Shirley I don't know.
Mary Don't talk to me about it, then.
Shirley There's nothing to talk about. He's got a headache alright?
Mary Unusual for him.
Shirley What's that meant to mean?
Mary Nothing.
Shirley There's nothing wrong with me.
Mary Just as well.
Shirley At least I've got a boyfriend. Oh, don't go.
Mary Like you say, at least you've got a boyfriend.
Shirley What's the matter?

Mary Nothing.
Shirley Come on, what is it?
Mary Nothing.
Shirley Men aren't everything you know, Mary.
Mary I know.

Steven enters

Steven Have you seen—there's a bloody great cargo ship just docked into the harbour.
Shirley And here we are, sat wasting our lives away. We could all go down and watch it for the day, that'd be a real thrill wouldn't it Mary.
Steven It's the biggest I've seen down there for years.
Mary I thought it was a tanker.
Steven And what would a tanker be doing here? It's a ship.
Mary What difference does it make? Could be a flying saucer for all I care.
Steven Because this is a fishing port, a timber port, a trawler port, a grain port, a working port, that's what this place is—it isn't all stupid pleasure boats and trips round the bay and amusement arcades and ice cream parlours and chip shops and funfairs and donkey rides and candy floss and bloody visitors and Cannon and Ball at the Floral Hall!
Shirley What do you know about cargo boats?
Steven My dad used to work on the cranes.
Mary How is your dad?
Steven Alright—we haven't heard. D'you want a coffee? They're having trouble getting post off the rigs. Do you?
Shirley Oh, alright.

Steven exits

Mary I feel mean now.
Shirley His dad couldn't even spell the word "crane", let alone use one—just something to piss on after the pub.
Mary His mother hasn't been out since he left her. I shouldn't have asked.
Shirley You're soft you. Now what?
Mary Nothing.
Shirley Where you going.
Mary I'll send you a postcard.

Scene 4

Mary exits

Paul and Billy enter

Paul You can't be trusted.
Billy I couldn't help it—I know that fruit machine, I couldn't lose.
Paul But you did.
Billy I hadn't put enough in.
Paul Go and get us a cappuccino.

Billy exits

Paul sits down

What's up with Mary?
Shirley What's it to you.
Paul I only asked.
Shirley Looks like rain.
Paul Maybe.
Shirley Did it rain much in London?
Paul About the same.
Shirley Must've been exciting living there.
Paul Yeah.
Shirley I wish I could do that, just get up and go somewhere else.
Paul Why don't you, then?
Shirley Wouldn't know where to start—I couldn't just leave Steven. What did you do in London?
Paul Oh, you know—this and that. What you doin' tonight?
Shirley Dunno yet.
Paul Corner of Trinity Road, eight-thirty.
Shirley You what?
Paul Don't be late, I'm not waiting.

Steven enters with drinks

Steven Here we are then.
Shirley I wanted a cappuccino.
Steven You've got coffee now.
Paul You can have mine when it comes.

Steven The prices, they should have two prices—one for visitors and one for the locals.
Paul Did you see Billy?
Steven Yeah, he's kicking shit out the fruit machine.
Paul Shit.

Paul exits

Steven What did he want?
Shirley We were just talking.
Steven I would've got cappuccino if you'd said.
Shirley This'll do now.

Mary enters

Mary Where's Paul and Billy?
Steven One armed Bandits. (*He squints his eyes and jerks his wrist up and down*)
Shirley Steven!
Steven Just trying to put a smile on Mary's face.

Nicky Tredwell and Shirt enter. They sit at another table

There's Nicky Tredwell and Shirt.
Mary That's it, I'm going.
Steven (*shouting*) Hello Nicky—how's it going then?
Nicky Reet enough. Now then Mary.

Paul and Billy enter

Billy It wasn't my fault—the machine's rigged.
Paul Well why put money in it then?
Shirley Sit down Mary.
Steven Did you know, Shirt's been done for breakin' and entering?
Mary He hasn't has he.
Shirley That's what he says.
Steven He has n' all. Haven't you Shirt?
Shirt You what?
Steven They caught him in the carpet department of Boyes. He set off the

Scene 4

alarm, so he rolls himself up into this great shag pile and waits, thinking he's safe like, but they brought dogs and sniffed him out.
Mary I'm going.
Billy I'm thirsty.
Shirley You're staying.
Steven Well I nearly pissed me'sen when I heard about it.
Paul It's your own fault, you beat up the fruit machine, the manager kicks us out, we don't have anything to drink.
Steven God you lot are miserable.
Billy I'll have this one. (*He picks up a coffee off the table*)
Mary No, don't...

Billy drinks

That's Nicky Tredwell's—he was here earlier.
Billy Cheers, Nicky.
Shirley You didn't talk to him, did you?
Mary No.
Shirt If I get sent down will you come and visit me?
Nicky No.
Shirt Me mam said she will.
Nicky Well she would.
Steven Why did you leave London?
Paul I'm on holiday.
Steven Wouldn't catch me living down there.
Mary I'd like to live there, wouldn't have time to get bored in London.
Billy I like London.
Steven You've never been there.
Shirley Neither have you.
Billy When we played Altrincham for the cup.
Steven So when are you going back?
Paul I dunno.
Billy He's got a girlfriend down there.
Steven Oh aye? Bit of a dark horse eh.

Steven pinches Paul's bottom

Paul Gerroff will you.
Shirley What's her name?

Billy Jay.
Shirley Pretty isn't it.

Ian enters, wearing sunglasses. He sits at a table at the back and reads a newspaper

Billy She might be coming to visit.
Paul Who says.
Billy Your postcard.
Steven Here, what's Soho like.
Shirley Steven.
Steven I'm just interested that's all. Is it like what you see on the telly—pouting girls sat round nearly naked in shop windows, all sex shops, massage parlours, strip shows and prostitutes—you'd be alright Shirley, if you got stuck for a bob or two.
Shirley What's that meant to mean.
Steven Nothing.
Shirley What about Mary.
Paul I'm going to buy a car while I'm up here.
Billy You haven't got any money.
Steven You haven't passed your test neither.
Paul So—who's gonna know.
Steven What if you have an accident.

Billy exits

Paul We won't—you're coming with me.
Steven You need someone who's qualified.
Paul You've had lessons haven't you.
Shirley We could all go for a drive in the country.
Mary Make a change from sitting round this place.
Steven I've only got a provisional.
Paul You don't have to come.
Steven Didn't say I wouldn't did I.
Shirley Why do you always have to spoil everything.
Steven I'll teach him to drive.
Nicky I'd like to see someone jump off that top board with all their clothes on.
Shirt Yeah.

Scene 4

Nicky Go on then—do it. Do it and I'll make it worth your while.
Shirt Oh aye.
Nicky Aye—I'll give you a packet of fags.
Mary Here look over there will you.
Steven (*shouting*) Hey Shirt how's the carpet business going?
Mary Flippin' heck, Shirley——
Nicky Sit down.
Mary Why don't you just walk over and ask to sit on his lap?
Shirley You said to look.
Steven Got any spare offcuts, me mam needs a new carpet.
Shirt I'll bloody twat thee one if tha don't watch it.
Steven Oh aye, you and whose army?
Shirt I wouldn't need one.
Nicky Just ignore the bugger and give us a fag.
Steven Come on——
Shirley Belt up Steven and look over there.
Steven Don't tell me what to do—bloody hell, what's Ian Smith doing here, thought he'd gone for good.
Mary You think he'd say hello.
Paul Where's Billy gone.
Shirley He just hasn't seen us that's all.
Steven Probably gone blind with too much——
Shirley Steven!
Steven Too much reading, it's bad for the eyes.
Mary Don't you ever think about anything else?
Steven No, I love books me.
Paul Where's Billy gone.

Shirt exits

Steven Where's blind dog Smith, been kidnapped by Indian take-away has it?
Mary He's put his paper down, he's picking up his bag, he's coming over—how's me mascara look?

Ian crosses over to them

Ian Hello—didn't see you all sat there.
Shirley I'm not surprised with them things on.

Mary You're back then?
Ian Yeah.
Steven What for?
Ian I live here.
Mary Good at college is it?
Ian Not bad, you know.
Steven You've gone skinhead?
Ian No.
Shirley Like the gear.
Mary Yeah, it's "Groovy".
Shirley D'you want a coffee?
Ian No—thanks but I was just off.
Mary You're different, ain't he Shirley?
Ian How d'you mean?
Mary You know, just different, it's the way you speak it's different.
Shirley Funny like.
Steven Posh.
Ian How's your dad getting on Steve?
Steven Alright.
Ian Still on the oil rigs is he?
Steven Yeah.
Ian Anyroad, I'd best be off.
Mary Maybe see you later.
Ian Aye.
Mary We could all go for a drink.
Ian Yeah why not. See you around.
Paul Yeah.

Ian exits

Mary God you're rude.
Steven Ponce. (*He gets up to go*)

Shirley follows him

Paul Where are you going?
Steven For a walk.
Shirley To watch the tide come in.
Steven Some of us have got to get back to work.

Scene 4

Paul Oh aye.
Steven Aye.

Steven pinches Shirley's bottom

Shirley Steven!
Steven Catch.

He throws Billy's ball to Paul. He spreads his hand over Shirley's bottom as they go to leave

Shirley Stop it will you.

They exit

Mary Oh no I've still got the key to the linen cupboard—she'll kill us.

Mary exits

Silence. A ship's bell rings in the distance

Shirt enters, soaking wet

Nicky puts a packet of ten fags on the table

Shirt What's this.
Nicky What's it look like.
Shirt You said a packet of fags.
Nicky That is a packet of fags.
Shirt They're half smoked.
Nicky I'll keep them if you want.

Billy enters

Billy I won I hit the jackpot I kicked it and the money just poured out. Where's everyone gone.
Paul To work.

Nicky and Shirt come over to Paul and Billy

Nicky Which one of them are you shagging.
Paul What's it to you.
Nicky This ball yours is it.
Billy No it's mine.
Paul All of them. I'm shagging them all.
Nicky You've been away haven't you. There's someone been looking for you down the Harbour Bar. Said they knew you from London—didn't they.
Shirt Oh aye London.
Nicky Showed us this photo of you stood in front of a statue. Said they were only up for the day.
Paul What did you say.
Nicky Why what've you done.
Paul I've missed you.

Scene 5

Men's changing room at the swimming pool

Paul is changing into trunks

Ian enters

Ian Excuse me…
Paul What.
Ian Paul.
Paul Yeah.
Ian How are you.
Paul Alright. What you doin' here.
Ian Swimming. I tried ringing after the other day.
Paul We haven't got a phone.
Ian Next door's.
Paul I'm not staying at home.
Ian Your mam said. Thought you were in London.
Paul I am—I'm just here for the summer.
Ian She didn't sound too bad.
Paul She's got pills. What did you want?
Ian The hair dryer's broke.

Scene 5

Paul They're always broken. Are you——
Ian Where do——
Paul You first.
Ian Where do you live in London?
Paul All over the place—with a friend.
Ian He must be loaded.
Paul Who says it's a he?
Ian Just thought that's all.
Paul Are you still into all that political stuff or have you grown up?
Ian What did you do in London?
Paul Grew up.

Pause

Ian D'you wanna go for a drink after?
Paul No.
Ian We could go down the *Bell*.
Paul I don't think there.
Ian Whatever pub you want, then.
Paul I said "no" didn't I?

Billy enters in luminous Bermudas

Billy Are you coming swimming or what? Hello Ian, you're home then, I heard you were.
Ian Aye.

Billy and Ian shake hands

Billy Nice to see you.
Paul Goodbye then.
Ian Yes, goodbye.

Ian exits

Billy Are you coming or not?
Paul Yeah.
Billy There's a letter come for you. It's from London.

Billy gives Paul the letter

Not a postcard is it.
Paul Did me mam bring it round?
Billy Yeah.
Paul What's she say.
Billy Nothing much, she was alright—just that someone keeps ringing for you and next door's getting pissed off. My phone keeps ringing n' all.
Paul Who is it.
Billy I dunno they keep putting phone down.
Paul I'll be out in a minute.
Billy I'm under the diving board.
Paul Billy.
Billy Cool, eh.

Billy exits

Paul puts the letter in a jeans pocket and exits

Scene 6

A pathway on the cliffside

Steven Anyway, I don't like him.
Shirley We're lost.
Steven It's a shortcut I promise, we'll come out over the South bay pool.
Shirley You're just jealous.
Steven Don't have to worry about him anyway.
Shirley How do you know?
Steven The manager called me over today, say's he reckons there's a full time job after the summer. Wants me to go over and help paint his house, as a favour like.
Shirley Bloody dogs.
Steven Did you hear me?
Shirley Yeah, you're gonna paint someone's house.
Steven I scratch his back, he'll scratch mine.
Shirley This manager, can he be trusted?
Steven Yeah, course—he's a laugh, more like one of the lads. What's that going on down there?
Shirley Morris dancers.

Scene 7

The swimming pool

Billy is sunbathing, Paul drying himself with a towel

Billy Move over, you're blocking the sun.
Paul Jesus, that's wicked—she shouldn't be allowed out with legs like that.
Billy Move will you.
Paul Put them on the side of a road and someone'd get killed.

Billy sits up

Billy Where?
Paul By the paddling pool.
Billy She's only about twelve.
Paul Don't be disgusting. The woman with her.
Billy She's ord enough to be your mam.
Paul I'm not looking at her face—it's the legs, look at them, I could get right up them, climb all the way up and eat her for dinner.
Billy Why don't you go over and ask her if you can borrow them for five minutes.
Paul I'd need all day.
Billy Go on, go and ask her if she wants a fuck.
Paul It's not the sort of thing you say to a complete stranger.
Billy You could take her to a hotel.
Paul I haven't got any money.
Billy She might have.
Paul I'm sunbathing.
Billy I'd keep an eye on the kid for you.
Paul No.
Billy Go on.
Paul No.
Billy Might make her 'oliday.
Paul What's that on your stomach?
Billy Where? (*He looks down at his stomach*)

Paul taps him on the nose as he does. Both lie back and sun themselves

Have you seen Rosemary Tredwell?

Paul No.
Billy Did she say anything?
Paul About what?
Billy I don't know.
Paul Then why ask?
Billy So she didn't say anything?
Paul What's there to say?
Billy Nothing. About you and her.
Paul What about me and her?
Billy Nothing.
Paul What's she been saying?
Billy I don't know.
Paul Come on, out with it.
Billy She said you tried to hypnotise her and it didn't work.
Paul It's not my fault she's got no imagination—stupid cow.
Billy You can't really hypnotise people.
Paul And levitate.
Billy I don't believe it. The whole body off the floor.
Paul You leave the body behind you idiot. I've left my body several times as a matter of fact.
Billy Where did you go to?
Paul Just into the world, that's all.
Billy What does it feel like?
Paul I can't describe it.
Billy Go on, try.
Paul I can't.
Billy I want to know.
Paul I can't.
Billy You were probably just dreaming.
Paul I could do it now if I wanted to.
Billy Go on then. Float up to the top board and back again.
Paul D'you want a Coke?
Billy You can't do it.
Paul I do it when I feel like it. Well do you or don't you?
Billy What?
Paul Want a Coke.
Billy I'll 'ave a lolly instead, strawberry.

Paul exits

Scene 7

Billy carries on sunning himself

Nicky and Shirt enter

Nicky Come on Billy, haven't you got anything to say?
Billy What's there to say?
Nicky About my sister.
Billy I don't know what you're talking about.
Nicky You and my sister.
Billy I haven't done anything.
Nicky I never said you had did I?
Billy No.
Nicky You've been seeing her.
Billy No I haven't.
Shirt Are you calling him a liar?
Billy No.
Shirt Then he must be telling the truth.
Nicky The changing rooms, now.
Billy I don't want to.
Nicky Scared.
Billy No I'm not.
Nicky Fight me.
Billy No.
Shirt He's scared.
Billy I don't believe in it, I don't believe in fighting.
Shirt Is that why you wear a cross?
Billy It's God.
Shirt He believes in God.
Nicky Shut up. Do you go to church?
Billy No—I don't think you have to. I mean if you don't go to church it doesn't mean you don't believe in Him, doesn't mean there isn't a God.
Nicky Come on, leave him alone.
Shirt You what?
Nicky I said leave him.

Paul enters with a lolly and an ice cream

Paul What do you want?
Nicky Listen, you queer bent bastard, tell him to leave my sister alone.

Paul What for?
Nicky No reason.
Paul What's all the fuss about, then?
Nicky Nothing.
Paul Go home Billy.
Billy Why?
Paul Go home will you.

Billy takes his lolly and exits

Nicky Think you're clever don't you.
Paul No.
Nicky Been to London.
Paul So?
Nicky Tell him to leave my sister alone, she's already spoke for—right.
Paul He hasn't been anywhere near her.
Nicky How do you know?
Paul Because he hasn't.
Nicky Tell him I don't like his face either.
Paul Don't go out with him then.
Nicky Who's been seeing my sister?
Paul How the bloody hell should I know. Could be anyone.
Nicky What's that mean?
Paul Nothing.
Nicky What you sayin' about my sister?
Paul Nothing.
Nicky Don't talk about my sister like that.
Paul Like what?
Nicky Like that.
Paul What?
Nicky Stop takin' the piss.
Paul I'm not.
Nicky You are.
Paul I'm not.
Nicky Bloody are.
Paul I'm not.
Nicky Bloody are.
Paul Bloody not.
Nicky Bloody are!

Scene 8

Paul sticks his ice cream in Nicky's face. Paul and Nicky fight. Shirt joins in

Billy and Ian enter. They join in

Scene 8

Shirley and Steven

Steven So where were you.
Shirley Out.
Steven Out where.
Shirley Just out that's all.
Steven What, on your own.
Shirley I went to the bingo.
Steven You hate the bingo.
Shirley Where the bloody hell are we Steven.
Steven Over the Spa.
Shirley I knew we should've stuck to the path.
Steven It's a shortcut I'm tellin' you. Hang on——

He grabs Shirley by the arm

Shirley What?
Steven You don't like the bingo.
Shirley Let go will you. I wasn't with anyone, right.
Steven Right. You smiled.
Shirley Oh don't be soft.

Steven goes to kiss her

   No.
Steven Come on.
Shirley We're lost.
Steven Go on.

They kiss

Shirley Stop it will you.

Steven What?
Shirley Breathing in me face like that.
Steven I can't help it, it's you—you get me going.
Shirley Suck on a mint then.
Steven You've got beautiful lips.
Shirley Give over.
Steven No, honest you have.

They kiss

Shirley Stop looking at your watch.
Steven I never.
Shirley I saw you.
Steven Just a bit pushed for time that's all—gotta get back for the three-thirty from Newbury.

Shirley exits

Shirley.

Scene 9

Billy's flat/bedsit. Ian is cleaning Paul's bloody nose with cotton wool

Ian (*shouting; off*) We'll need more water.
Paul What are you doing?
Ian Try not to speak.
Paul Don't tell me what to do—ouch, my nose.
Ian I said not to speak.
Paul You hurt me.

Billy enters with water and cotton wool

Billy I've only got liquid detergent.
Paul I'm not a bloody germ you know.

Ian dabs at Paul's nose

Leave off.

Scene 9

Ian Do you want this cleaned or not?
Paul No. (*He looks in the shaving mirror*) I'm scarred for life, it'll never go down that won't.
Ian You're magnifying it.
Paul Enjoying this aren't you?

Ian turns the mirror round

Ian It's just a cut that's all.
Paul Be different if it was your nose, we'd have had the plastic surgeon here by now.
Billy I get spots worse than that.
Paul Thanks Billy.
Ian Stop going on will you, you're givin' me headache.
Paul I just got me head kicked in that's all, sorry about the fuss, I'll be right as rain by tea—get him an aspirin Billy, doesn't matter about me.
Ian You sound just like your mam.
Paul You leave my mam out of this. At least when she worked in a pub she only pulled the pints.
Billy You'd be in hospital but for him.
Paul So?
Billy I think you should say thank you.
Paul Thank you. And what about me, don't I get any thanks?
Billy They weren't going to touch me.
Paul No?
Billy No. Told them I believed in God.
Paul You what?
Billy Said I believed in God.
Paul You're lying.
Billy I do.
Paul You're telling me I got this for nothing? That Nicky Tredwell left you alone because he's soft in the head about God?
Billy Just as you came, they were going.
Paul Where to, church? Where are you going?
Billy To get some disinfectant.
Paul No, don't go.
Billy I want to.

Billy exits

Ian Your hair's shorter.
Paul I've been disfigured.
Ian Come here, I'll give it another wipe. I said come here.

Paul does as he is told

> God you're stubborn. Short hair suits you. Remember that time you had your hair shaved and they made you wear a tin helmet to school till it had grown back?

Paul So?
Ian I just remembered that's all.
Paul My eyes hurt.
Ian Sit down.
Paul I want to stand up.
Ian Stand up then.
Paul Stop telling me what to do, you're always telling me what to do.
Ian Sorry.
Paul And don't apologise.
Ian I'll go if you want.
Paul Piss off. Throw us me jeans. Just give us me jeans.

Ian picks up Paul's jeans. The letter drops out. Ian throws Paul the jeans

> And the letter.

Ian looks at the letter

> Give it here will you.

Ian gives Paul the letter. Paul puts the letter in his jeans pocket

Ian What are you getting dressed for. It's from London. You don't have to get dressed.
Paul I'll hit you if you don't stop it. Where are my shoes.
Ian Going somewhere.
Paul I just want to know where my shoes are that's all.

Ian throws Paul his shoes

> Ta. (*He puts his shoes on*)

Scene 11

Ian From a friend is it. Your letter.
Paul Don't start right just don't start.
Ian I'm not starting anything I'm only asking——
Paul Don't I said don't.
Ian Why don't you stop feeling so bloody sorry for yourself and do something for once.
Paul Yeah. The only person you've ever loved is yourself. You walk round with a mirror forever held up to your face. (*He holds out the shaving mirror to Ian*) Go on take it.
Ian I have to go.
Paul Yeah.
Ian Come on I'll buy you a drink.
Paul No.

SCENE 10

Billy's flat

Billy is holding a letter over the spout of a boiling kettle, trying to steam it open

The door bell rings. It rings again, long and insistent

Billy Shit. (*He goes to answer the door and leaves the kettle boiling*)

SCENE 11

Night-time

Paul and Shirley

Paul On a clear night you can see for miles, round the coast in either direction.
Shirley Pity about the fog.
Paul It's beautiful.
Shirley Is that the lighthouse?
Paul You don't have to see something to know it's there.

Shirley Just as well. I'm short sighted. What's your girlfriend in London like?
Paul Alright.
Shirley Is she pretty?
Paul Yeah, suppose.
Shirley What, don't you know?
Paul She's pretty, yeah. If you wanted to kill yourself this is the bridge to do it off—you'd have a great view, all the way out to sea. I'd do it in broad daylight.
Shirley Is that how I make you feel?
Paul Shout something.
Shirley No.
Paul Go on.
Shirley Someone might come.
Paul You can do anything you want up here.
Shirley What do you want to do?
Paul Chuck you off this bridge.

He tries to pick her up

Shirley No don't, put me down.

They kiss. She pulls back

Paul What's wrong?

Scene 12

Billy's flat: the same setting as at the end of Scene 10

The kettle is still boiling

Billy and Ian enter

Billy runs over and turns the kettle off. He burns his hand

Billy I was just making a cup of tea.
Ian Run it under some cold water.

Scene 12

Billy exits

Ian picks up the letter and looks at it

Billy enters

Billy It's Paul's.
Ian You've spilt water on it.
Billy I was making a cup of tea.
Ian Show me your hand.

Billy shows him

Billy It's from London.
Ian Must be important. What did he do in London?
Billy Dunno. He's taking me back with him. He didn't say when he'd be back.
Ian I was just passing. There's hardly room to swing a cat in here—he could stay with his mum and dad.
Billy They don't get on—he thumped his dad, something to do with his mam I think. I get lonely, I like living with someone.
Ian Show me your hand again.

Billy does so

  You've got nice hands.
Billy I wear gloves a lot. I have to, I'm on jam doughnuts. You won't tell Paul about the letter. (*He takes the letter from Ian*)

Paul enters

Billy puts the letter in his pocket

Ian I was just passing. How's the nose?
Paul Alright.
Billy I'll make us a cup of tea eh.
Ian Billy was just sayin' you're takin' him back to London with you when you go. (*He pauses*) I'll maybe see you then.
Paul Maybe.

Ian goes to leave

Give us a ring tomorrow.

Ian exits

Billy How long's he back for?
Paul I dunno.
Billy Anyroad, better get to bed—I've gotta be up early.
Paul What time d'you finish?
Billy Three.
Paul See you down the caff then.
Billy Yeah, alright.
Paul You have the bed tonight. I'll make do with the couch.
Billy I don't mind.
Paul Have the bed Billy.
Billy Alright.
Paul Here, there's nothing in you and Rosemary Tredwell is the?
Billy What d'you think I am, stupid?
Paul Night then.
Billy Night.

Billy exits

Paul takes out a letter from his jeans pocket and opens it. A ten pound note drops out. He pockets it and reads the letter. Then he turns on the radio. Pop music is heard. He picks up the phone and dials

Paul (*softly*) Hello, Jim?... It's me... Me... No, I'm not in London... Listen... A radio... I dunno, soon... I told you... Listen... Yeah I got the letter... No, I don't want you to send me the train fare... Listen to me will you. I don't want you to write anymore... Because I don't... No, don't ring, you can't—I'm not at that number anymore——

Loud slam of a door. Paul slams down the receiver and burns the letter

Billy enters with a glass

Billy What's that burning.

Scene 13

Paul Nothing, just me fag caught on a bit of paper that's all.
Billy You wanna give up smoking you do, it's bad for you.
Paul Yeah.
Billy It is.
Paul I know.
Billy Next door are at it again.
Paul Yeah.
Billy I'll get a glass of water then.

The phone rings

   Who's that?
Paul I don't know, leave it.
Billy Might be important.
Paul Leave it—they'll ring back if it is.

The phone keeps ringing. Billy answers it

   I'm not here.
Billy Hello? Hello—is anyone there? (*He puts the phone down*)
Paul Who was it.
Billy I dunno, they put phone down.

Scene 13

The cliffside

Ian enters, running

Paul enters

Paul I give up.
Ian Come on.

Paul falls to the ground

   You smoke too much.
Paul It's the air I'm not used to all this air. Anyway I touched you.

Ian No you never.
Paul I did.
Ian You didn't.
Paul I did.

Ian sits next to Paul. Paul tags him and jumps up

Ian Right.
Paul And no cheating this time.
Ian I don't cheat.

Ian chases Paul. They dodge and swerve

Paul You and that bloke—you never did did you. Both at the same time.
Ian One after the other.
Paul You dirty bugger.
Ian You're going to pay.
Paul For what.
Ian Everything.

Ian brings Paul down with a rugby tackle

Paul Cheat that's cheating you're only meant to touch. You always did cheat that's how come you got to that school.
Ian Have you ever thought about dying.
Paul Fuck off. What—what you laughing at.
Ian You—you're bloody ugly.

They both laugh

Paul So what am I going to pay for.
Ian I don't know what have you done.

Billy enters

Billy I love the smell of rubber. Can you smell it?
Paul Let's have a look at your forehead. Come on show us. Screw up your face.

Ian screws up his face and Paul feels the lines on his forehead

Scene 14

Billy Copper says people have been coming from all over.
Ian (*to Paul*) Give over.
Billy You can see right inside—half the front room just gone slipped slipped down the cliffside and into the sea. There's a sideboard smashed into a tree half way down and sheets a load of white sheets everywhere.
Ian It won't be long before all this has gone and people will look back and say "They were cavemen fucking cavemen".
Paul Got any sweets Billy.
Ian It's over.
Paul What's this.
Billy I like Black Jacks.
Ian It's all slipping away.
Billy Want a goodie. Come on, let's see if we can get any nearer.
Paul Get a better view on the telly.
Billy You're not coming then. So you're staying. I'll see thee later.

Billy exits

Paul I want a car.
Ian What for.
Paul I'd just get in it and drive anywhere. I wouldn't stop till I had to then I'd turn round and just keep on going.
Ian You wouldn't get a mile before you killed yourself.
Paul I can drive.
Ian Oh aye.
Paul Yeah.
Ian Get off.
Paul What's slipping away.
Ian Nothing.
Paul It's only a bloody hotel you know.
Ian We did you know—he went first while I waited at the foot of the bed then when he finished I took over.

Scene 14

The café

Mary is waiting

Nicky and Shirt enter. Shirt carries a bunch of flowers

Nicky Hello Mary.
Mary There's someone sitting there.
Nicky You never had to wait for me Mary.
Mary Who says I'm waiting?

Nicky and Shirt sit. Shirt puts his feet up on the table

Nicky Behave yourself.

Shirt takes his feet off the table

Shirt Scared someone might think you're still going out with him?
Mary Doesn't bother me Nicky Tredwell.
Nicky G'ez another coffee Shirt.
Shirt You've got one.
Nicky So—I want another.
Shirt I haven't got any money.
Mary Nice flowers.
Shirt They're for me mam; d'you think she'll like them?

Shirley and Steven enter

Nicky See you later.

Nicky and Shirt move to another table

Steven I wouldn't go if I didn't have to.
Shirley I'm not stopping you am I?
Steven I don't want to go.
Shirley Don't then.
Mary If you two are gonna argue I'm going.
Shirt D'you think she'll like them?
Nicky No.
Steven Shirley.
Shirley Yes Steven.
Steven What are you gonna do tonight then?
Shirley I don't know, wash me hair.
Mary I wish something'd just happen, something big like an earthquake.
Shirley You're always bored you.

Scene 14

Mary That's because everything's boring.
Steven I'm never bored me.
Shirley Shut up Steven.
Nicky Thought you didn't have any money.
Shirt I don't; I found them.
Nicky Oh, yeah.
Shirt Yeah, outside a shop.
Mary We could go and see a play.
Shirley What for?
Mary It'd be different—we could go to the one on Valley Bridge, I've always wanted to go there.
Shirley I've been, we went with the school.
Mary I never did. What was it like?
Shirley Alright—it was something about dead posh people without any scenery, then they took us to see Orville the Duck at the Futurist and we had a really good laugh.
Mary Come on let's go, we could get dressed up and make a night out of it.
Steven Yeah.
Shirley Thought you were painting your boss's house.
Steven So, doesn't stop you from going does it.
Mary Come on, it'll be fun.
Steven What else are you going to do?
Shirley Go for a drink with Tom Cruise.
Nicky You haven't told her yet have you?
Shirt No.
Nicky She'll hit the fuckin' roof, use your gob as a vase for those flowers, you'll need plastic surgery when she's done.
Shirt Yeah—but I think she'll like them.

Paul and Ian enter

Nicky and Shirt exit

Mary We're going to the theatre tonight, to see a play.
Paul Oh aye.
Shirley It's not decided.
Ian What are you going to see.
Mary Whatever they've got on I suppose.

Ian You want to ring first, they might be booked out.
Steven I suppose you know all about it. They'll get in.
Ian Might not.
Steven Hard day at the library was it?
Shirley Steven.
Steven Well, I bet he's never been.
Mary Of course he has.
Steven When?
Ian A while back.
Steven He hasn't been.
Paul What d'you want to go and see a play for anyway?
Shirley It's Mary that wants to go.
Mary I'll go on me own, you don't have to come.
Steven She wants to.
Ian I was ten, me mam was doing the coats and I had to go with her, they sat me at the back with an orange and a packet of crisps—it was an amateur production of *Waiting for Godot* by Samuel Beckett.
Steven Told you he hadn't been.

Ian exits

Mary I'll ring them. Don't fancy coming do you?
Paul No thanks. I've already got something on.
Steven Oh aye, pretty is she?
Paul Yeah.
Steven Must be short sighted then. Here, have you heard about Patsi?
Mary This another of your daft stories is it.
Steven No.
Shirley Yes.
Mary I'll call you later.
Steven Wait on, I'll walk with you. It's his parrot, it's left him—he goes home one night and there's a note stuck to it's perch sayin' "Get Stuffed"——
Paul Get away.
Mary I'm going.
Steven Hang on—it's true, honest—the cage door wide open and a window smashed—he reported it kidnapped and came down the pub ballin' his eyes out, bloody woman, you could see why the parrot left——

Scene 14

Mary Are you coming or not?
Steven They say he dressed it in a tutu.
Paul So who wrote the note?
Mary I'm going.
Steven Alright, you've got no sense of humour you lot—miserable sods.

Mary and Steven exit

Shirley He knows.
Paul What does he know.
Shirley He keeps going on.
Paul He doesn't know, he knows nothing.
Shirley Someone's told him.
Paul There's nothing to tell, we haven't done anything. (*He puts his arm round her*) Don't worry eh.

Ian enters

Shirley I'll see you later.
Paul Yeah.

Shirley exits

Ian What's all that about then?
Paul All what.
Ian He'll have you if he finds out.
Paul Finds out what? D'you think she fancies me then.
Ian I'm telling you he'll have you.
Paul Shut up and have a fag.
Ian You haven't changed have you.
Paul Have a fag.
Ian I've given up.
Paul C'mon, let's go and see Ray, get some stuff and go up the castle.
Ian We haven't got any money.
Paul I thought you had money.
Ian Not enough for that.
Paul He'll give us some.
Ian No he won't.
Paul Yeah he will, he's always flush in the summer Ray, he'll give us a joint.

Ian I don't fancy it.
Paul What's up?
Ian Nothing. Let's go swimming.
Paul You go swimming. How much money have you got?

Ian takes some change out of his pocket

Ian One pound sixty-three.
Paul Go an' get us a Kit Kat—I'll pay you back later, go on—look at her pushing the pram.
Ian The bloke's better looking.
Paul I'm not looking at him am I. Go on.

Ian exits

(*He shouts*) Get your'sen a Mars, if you like.

Scene 15

The beach at night. Paul and Billy

Billy She's not coming.
Paul I'm going to buy a Ford Zodiac—I like the fins. Leopard skin seats and big fluffy dice—what do you think.
Billy I don't think this is right doing it behind his back like this. She's still his girlfriend.
Paul It's her choice she doesn't have to come.
Billy Why couldn't we have met her in a pub.
Paul I like the beach.
Billy Rosemary Tredwell didn't.
Paul Forget the dice I'll have a nodding dog instead. She's been asking for you.
Billy Who. What's she say.
Paul I think she fancies you.
Billy Well I don't want to see her.
Paul You should've given her one the other week when you had the chance.
Billy Why didn't you. She's not coming. I don't know what you see in her.

Scene 15

Paul Long legs, fishnet stockings, a tight little black leather mini skirt with a zip running up the back, riding all the way up to her knickers.
Billy She doesn't dress like that.
Paul You haven't seen her in bed.
Billy Neither have you.
Paul Haven't I?
Billy No. Liar.
Paul Up here, I've seen it all up here, I've shagged her a thousand times already.
Billy So why do you need to go out with her.

Shirley enters, carrying her shoes

Shirley What's he doing here?
Billy I'd best be off.
Paul Hang on. It's alright, he won't say anything.
Shirley Why, what have we done?
Billy Look, I don't want to cause any trouble.
Paul Shirley——
Shirley Don't touch me.
Paul I didn't, I just want you to feel better.
Shirley What do you think you are, a bottle of aspirin?
Paul I don't understand, why did you come?
Shirley To watch an eclipse of the moon, that's what you said. You never go anywhere without him.
Paul He's my friend; you don't like it, go home.
Shirley What if he tells Steve?
Paul He won't, will you?
Billy Tell who, what?
Paul Come on, don't be angry.

Shirley goes over to Billy and gives him a long slow kiss on the lips

Billy What was that for?
Shirley Paul.
Billy I've never seen an eclipse of the moon before.
Shirley You don't see anything, that's the point, everything just goes dark for a minute.
Paul It's not like that.

Shirley Come on, give us a smile; I'm staying aren't I? If you don't like it, go home.
Billy What do we do when it happens?
Paul We don't have to do anything—just watch it go red.
Shirley I should've brought me space suit.
Billy We could light a bonfire.
Paul Why?
Billy I dunno, burn summat, be like joining in; that's what they did in the old days isn't it?
Paul That's stupid.
Shirley He's no fun is he Billy?

She kisses Paul on the cheek

I'm sorry.
Paul You're embarrassing Billy.
Billy No she's not.

Shirley kisses Billy on the cheek and runs her hand through his hair

Shirley He's got lovely hair our Billy hasn't he?
Paul You're drunk.
Shirley Just a couple of gins that's all, with Steve before he went... This isn't right... I shouldn't be here... He's painting his boss's house tonight.

Paul picks up one of Shirley's shoes

Paul Hey Billy, catch.

He throws the shoe to Billy

Over here, come on.

Billy and Paul throw the shoe to each other

Shirley No, don't.
Paul Watch out for the sea Billy.
Shirley Give me the shoe Billy.

Scene 15

Paul Come on Shirley, come and get it.

Shirley dives for the shoe

Shirley It's not fair, there's two of you——
Paul That's how you play.

Shirley dives at Paul. He throws the shoe to Billy and grabs her. They roll over and over

Shirley Stop it, I'm dizzy, there's sand in my hair, I'll be sick.

They stop. Shirley is on top of Paul. She laughs

We can't leave Billy. (*She rolls off Paul*)
Billy I don't mind.
Shirley Besides, I want to see the eclipse. I 'ate the beach, I always 'ave, ever since I were a kid.
Billy Listen.
Paul To what?
Billy The sea.
Shirley I haven't got the right body for it.
Paul What?
Shirley The beach.
Paul Don't be soft, you look great.
Shirley I'm too fat.
Paul No you're not.
Shirley I am.
Paul You're not.
Shirley I am.
Paul She's got a smashing body 'asn't she Billy.
Billy Yeah.
Shirley You're just saying that.
Paul No I'm not—you look bloody great in a bikini.
Shirley Bet you say that to all the girls.
Paul No.
Billy He said it to Rosemary Tredwell the other week.
Paul No I didn't.
Billy Yes you did.

Paul Lying get.
Shirley He didn't?

Pause

Billy He did.

Paul chases Billy. Billy dodges and jumps on Paul's back and rides him like a bronco

   Yeehaaaa!
Shirley Ride him Billy.
Paul Gerroff.
Billy Bring me the head of Alfredo Garcia!
Paul Stop it.
Billy See how the gringo devil squeals.
Shirley Let's bury him in the sand.
Billy Up to his neck.
Paul You're choking me.
Shirley And leave his head for the crabs to chew on.

Paul flicks Billy violently over his shoulder, throwing him to the ground

Paul Clumsy bloody idiot, he was choking me.
Shirley He was playing.

She helps Billy to sit up

Paul That's his trouble, he never knows when to stop.
Shirley Leave him alone.
Paul Since when have you been his friend?
Billy I'm fine, really.

Shirley backs off

Shirley How much longer do we have to wait? It's cold, I'm cold—and that wasn't an invitation for you to put your mucky paws round me.
Paul Why don't you go for a swim Billy?
Billy We could all go.

Scene 15

Shirley And freeze to death.
Billy Come on it'll be fun.
Paul Shirley's right—you go, we'll just sit here and watch, won't we?
Shirley Will we?
Paul Only if you want to.
Billy Once you're in you can't feel the cold.
Paul We don't want to Billy.
Billy It's no fun on your own.
Paul You can't force us!
Shirley There's no need to bite his head off.
Billy I'll go for a swim. (*He undresses down to his underpants*) You won't go?
Shirley Of course not.
Billy If you do you'll leave my clothes behind?
Paul Yes.

Billy exits

Shirley What did he mean by that?
Paul Don't ask me.
Shirley Funny you are: up one minute, down the next, like a Yo-Yo.
Paul I just don't like it here that's all.
Shirley It was your idea.
Paul Anyroad, come the end of the season and I'll be gone—might go to Torquay.
Shirley What d'you want to go there for?
Paul They've got palm trees.
Shirley You're mad.

Pause

Paul Have you ever been hypnotised? Lie down and I'll make you float. I can.
Shirley Get away.
Paul Just lie down and trust me.

She lies down

Shirley And no funny business.

Paul Close your eyes.

Shirley They are. Now what? I can't keep them closed forever.

Paul Clench your fists tight, tighter, grit your teeth and screw up your face—till your whole body's tense, rigid——

Shirley It is.

Paul Now hold it.

Shirley It hurts.

Paul Good. Now let go, let it all out, feel your body sinking into the sand ... all that pain draining away ... sinking ... deeper and deeper ... till there's nothing ... nothing ... nothing...

Silence. Paul circles her body

Shirley.

Silence. Paul kneels and leans forward to kiss her. Shirley slaps his face

Shirley Don't stop.

Paul stands up sharp

Paul You're floating ... drifting... Count backwards from a hundred ... there's nothing in your head ... it's completely empty... Floating ... all you can hear is the sound of my voice ... forever ... without words ... floating ... without pain...

Silence

Shirley. Can you hear me Shirley.

Silence. Paul kneels, puts his hands on her ribcage and rubs upwards to her breasts. He hesitates

Shirley Don't stop.

He kisses her. She frantically undoes his trousers while he pushes her skirt up. After a while Paul rolls off

What's wrong?

Scene 16

Paul We can't.
Shirley Why not?
Paul There's no protection. I haven't got any.
Shirley It's alright.
Paul It's not safe!
Shirley Is it Steven?
Paul I think you should go home.
Shirley I'll be seeing you then.
Paul Yeah.

Shirley exits

Billy enters naked

Billy Where's Shirley?

Paul laughs

Scene 16

The café

Mary (*shrilly*) "Don't talk to the guests Mary, it's rude", it's not as if I could, even if I wanted to, they're all Japanese. How dare she speak to me like that in front of everyone—she's never liked me. All I said was "Sianora".
Shirley Do you want this doughnut?
Mary What were you doing last night?
Shirley Watching a video.
Mary She's no right to speak to me like that.
Shirley It's her hotel.
Mary Just because people take to me—she's like a block of ice. Guests are always giving me things, she can't stand it—these Japanese keep on leaving me presents.
Shirley Like what?
Mary Nothing special. Tea-bags.
Shirley Tea-bags?
Mary From Japan.

Shirley I wouldn't be jealous of that.
Mary You can't buy them in the shops.
Shirley I'd rather have their money. You should get another job—I wouldn't like to change other people's dirty sheets all day.
Mary Nobody's asking you to.
Shirley You should do what I do, people are always glad to see me.
Mary Especially the men.
Shirley They book in, they book out, I smile and that's all.
Mary It's not me—flirting with other women's husbands all day.
Shirley I don't flirt, I'm paid to smile: the bigger the smile the better the tip.
Mary I couldn't do it.
Shirley No—it's not everyone can be a receptionist.
Mary I'd feel daft—like one of those flippin' stupid donkeys over there—all dressed up with nowhere to go, silly great grin stuck on me face.
Shirley I don't feel like a donkey.
Mary I wish I could just run away.
Shirley You could go to Birmingham.
Mary I'd just go and I wouldn't stop.
Shirley That's where Steve's dad ran off to, the Black Country with Mrs Curran.
Mary It's his mum I feel sorry for—after all those years and the man you love runs off with another woman.
Shirley She let herself go.
Mary Fancy running away to Birmingham. I mean when you think about running away it's to somewhere exotic, somewhere warm, somewhere exciting, not Birmingham.
Shirley It's probably all they could afford, about as far as their imaginations could stretch.
Mary Have you seen Paul?
Shirley No.
Mary I think he's quite exotic, the way he keeps going off.
Shirley Look at him over there, the one with Union Jack shorts——
Mary I quite fancy him actually.
Shirley He's got a face like a melted-down wellington boot.
Mary No he hasn't.
Shirley What d'you call them cheeks then? (*She sucks in her cheeks*) Wouldn't catch me kissin' that, all those spots, catch blackheads.
Mary Not off Paul you wouldn't.

Scene 16

Shirley What's Paul got to do with it?
Mary I fancy him.
Shirley So why tell me, tell him—what do I want to know who you fancy for?
Mary There's no need to get short.
Shirley You hardly know him.
Mary I've known him since junior school.
Shirley You're wasting your time.
Mary How do you know?
Shirley He's not your sort.
Mary That's for me to decide. I don't tell you what to think about Steven, do I?
Shirley That's different, I don't pretend to love him. You're just soft you are, always falling in love, always getting hurt. You're too old for love.
Mary That what you think is it?
Shirley Yeah.
Mary Right.
Shirley Right.
Mary I thought you were me mate.
Shirley I am, that's why I'm tellin' you. Where's Steven?
Mary How should I know.

Paul enters

Paul Hello.
Mary Hello Paul.
Paul I'll get a drink then. D'you want anything?
Shirley No ta.
Mary Yes please—cappuccino, no sugar.

Paul exits

Shirley Gets right up my nose the way he goes on about having no money, no job—all he does is lie around on the beach all day—he's never had a proper job.
Mary What about your Scott, when was the last time he had a job?
Shirley That's different, it's his nerves.
Mary Oh aye?
Shirley Yeah, he's got a doctor's note.

Mary What about that chip shop he painted?
Shirley No sugar, since when haven't you taken sugar?
Mary I'm on a diet.
Shirley What for?
Mary No, you're right—it's not me that should be watching me figure, is it.

Steven enters

Steven And how are my favourite girls tonight?
Shirley Belt up, Steven, you're late and I'm going home.
Steven What about the pictures?
Shirley Stuff the pictures.

Paul enters with cappuccinos

Paul Now then Steve.
Steve Now then.
Shirley So you're gonna talk to him all night are you?
Steven No.
Shirley I thought we were going to the pictures.
Steven You just said you were off.

Shirley exits

Shirley!

Steven exits

Paul What's up with her?
Mary Dunno. Thanks. What you doing tonight?
Paul Go for a drink with Billy.
Mary You've caught the sun.
Paul Aye, there's been a lot of it.
Mary It suits you. I haven't been to the pictures for ages. It's no fun on your own is it? Shirley and Steven are always going.
Paul You should go with them then.
Mary I'd feel like a gooseberry; 'sides, you never know when they're going to have an argument. The last film I went to see was *Lethal Weapon II*, it were dead good. Have you seen it?

Scene 16

Paul Yeah.
Mary They've got *III* on at the Opera House.
Paul Have they.
Mary Yeah.
Paul I saw it in London.
Mary Oh.

Ian enters with two bags of chips

Ian Here you go.
Paul Ta.

Ian and Paul open the bags of chips

Ian D'you want one?
Paul Ah what——
Mary No thanks.
Paul They've got vinegar on.
Ian So?

Paul and Ian eat the chips. Silence

Mary Hot isn't it?
Paul Too hot.
Ian You could fry an egg on the bonnet of a car like they do in the desert.
Mary Who does?
Ian The Army.
Paul Bollocks.
Ian Don't you want them?
Paul They've got vinegar on, I don't like vinegar.
Ian You should've said.
Paul You know I don't like vinegar.
Ian You should've said.
Paul I didn't think I had to.
Ian Here, have mine.
Paul I don't want yours.
Ian Have them they've got nothing on.
Paul I like them with salt.
Mary I'll see you later then.

Paul Where you going?
Mary Work—I have to. Thanks for the cappuccino.

Mary exits

Ian She fancies you.
Paul You know I don't like vinegar.
Ian Give over will you for Christ' sakes I'm not your bloody mam. Go and get another portion then it's only a packet of chips.
Paul I'll make do with these.
Ian If you don't like vinegar don't have vinegar.
Paul I'll eat these.

They eat. Pause. Paul pushes his chips away

Ian I'm thinking of going.
Paul What's stopping you?
Ian No, I mean going away. We could go together.
Paul I'm on holiday.
Ian Think about it eh.
Paul Pack it in.
Ian What?
Paul Tellin' us what to do.
Ian I know what you did in London.
Paul Yeah?
Ian Yeah—there's someone down there.

Paul screws up his chips

Why won't you tell us.
Paul There's nothing to tell. (*He throws his chips away*)

SCENE 17

A pub

Nicky and Shirt stand holding pool cues

Nicky Your shot.

Scene 17

Pause

    Just do it will you.
Shirt I'm thinking.
Nicky They don't respond to telepathy.
Shirt I can't decide which ball to hit.
Nicky It doesn't matter.
Shirt Why not?
Nicky Because you're a shit player.
Shirt Pool's not my game that's all, I can't work out the angles.

Steven enters

Nicky blocks his way

Steven Shove off will you.
Nicky Please.
Steven I haven't got time for games.
Shirt Why, what's up?
Steven Nothing.
Nicky Need any help?
Steven Just move will you.
Nicky Lookin' for someone?
Steven No.
Shirt Where's Shirley then.
Steven Look you've got summat to say say it or get out the way.
Nicky Giving you a spot of bother is she.
Steven No.
Nicky Out for a drink on your own eh. Sit down have a drink with us. Have you decided which ball to hit yet. Take a seat doesn't cost 'owt.

Steven sits

    Not in a hurry are you. So, how's it going.
Steven Alright.
Shirt You've snookered me.
Nicky Just hit the ball will you. He's having trouble deciding which ball to hit. D'you like pool.
Steven It's alright.

Nicky I don't like it down South. Miserable lot all out for their sen. I've been there. You can see it just by going on the Tube—nobody laughs. Up here we're different we all stick together—one fights we all fight one doesn't fight—we make him see sense. Don't go Steven.
Steven I'm not.
Nicky Good.
Steven Why d'you pick a fight with Billy and Paul?
Nicky Why not?
Shirt Just a friendly scrap, that's all.
Steven It's been nice talking then.
Nicky You've not heard anything about our Rosemary have you?
Steven No—should I have.
Shirt I can't do it, there's not a ball I can hit.
Nicky Go off the bloody cushion then. This is just between you and me right. She's foolin' around with someone and Paddy only just gone to Belfast. So if you hear of anything you'll tell us won't you?
Steven Yeah, course.
Nicky I don't approve of that, fellas messin' round with other bloke's birds behind their back.
Steven What you gonna do about it?
Nicky What would you do if you found out Shirley was carrying on?
Steven She's not.
Nicky But just supposing.
Shirt Smart looking lass, lot of blokes I know wouldn't mind——
Nicky Shut it eh.
Steven I should knock his block off for even suggesting it.
Nicky Just take your shot. But what would you do?
Steven I'd kill the bastard.
Nicky We could give you a hand if you like.
Steven I wouldn't need help.
Nicky Aye, but what if he had friends? That's what happened with Billy, his friends got in the way. Here, you don't fancy givin' us a hand do you—seein' how we'd help you out if you were in trouble?
Steven No.
Nicky Aye, mates of yours aren't they.
Steven What, you think it's Billy?
Nicky I dunno.
Steven Why don't you just ask her.
Nicky And you think she'd say?

Steven Ask her if there's anything goin' on, ask her if it's Billy, ask her straight to her face you'd know if she was lying.
Shirt And even if she said "no" it wouldn't prove anything would it.
Nicky And we'd lose the element of surprise—she'd know that we know and likewise this fella. No, we'll just watch. See who she talks to, how she behaves, soon be able to tell who it is. Meanwhile I'm gonna thump Billy for it. So if you hear anything you'll let us know.
Steven Yeah.
Nicky And don't forget, if ever you need any help.
Steven Aye, thanks.

Steven exits

SCENE 18

Ian and Paul. Ian is lying on his back with his knees up. A bottle of cider is between them

Ian It doesn't matter——
Paul Oh no, you're not going to start are you.
Ian Whatever position you're in the whole world's spinning.
Paul Just shut up and look.

Ian sings

Ian I know all the words just can't get them in the right order. (*He sings loudly*) Whey—a—whey—hey!
Paul That's Corrigans those lights.
Ian We could go for a game of bingo.
Paul I hate this place in winter.
Ian Yeah no Max Jaffa at the Spa or Little 'n' Large to cheer us all up.
Paul He's dead now.
Ian Who?
Paul Max Jaffa.
Ian They're all dead.
Paul Just give us a drink.
Ian If I said, right now, anything you want, you can change it what would it be.

Paul I give in, what's the answer?
Ian Close your eyes, imagine the world——
Paul Do I have to?
Ian Go on.

Paul closes his eyes

  What can you see.
Paul A room. A big room. With a door.
Ian What can you see.
Paul The door.
Ian What else.
Paul Nothing, it's dark.
Ian Open the door.
Paul It's locked.
Ian Turn on the bloody light then.
Paul The bulb's broke.
Ian You're bloody useless you are.
Paul What if you don't want to change anything.
Ian Here have a drink.

They both swig from the bottle

Paul What about the sea?
Ian Take a saucepan——
Paul I always hate it when you get like this.
Ian Come on.
Paul I don't want to.
Ian You've given up.
Paul When you said a drink I thought you meant a pint.
Ian Why won't you argue with us.
Paul Because I don't understand what you're saying half the time.
Ian Fuck off. See this arm—whose arm d'you think that is.
Paul I don't know looks like yours.
Ian That's what I thought for all these years—then the other day I looked down and they weren't my arms anymore.
Paul Whose are they then.
Ian I looked down and saw my father's arms hanging off me—don't you see—there's no escape you can't just run away it goes with you.

Scene 18

Paul I don't care—I don't give a fuck about anything. (*He takes out a lighter and holds his palm over it*)
Ian You need petrol if you're gonna do it properly.
Paul Yeah—you'd buy it for us 'n' all wouldn't you.
Ian Only if you give us the money.

Paul holds his palm over the flame until he can't stand it anymore

Paul Shit!
Ian Let me see.
Paul Piss off.
Ian Show me.

Ian grabs Paul's hand and pours cider over it

Paul Now lick it off.

Ian kisses Paul. Paul pulls away

Ian What's the matter.
Paul I don't want to.
Ian Why not.
Paul Because I don't.
Ian You've never not wanted to before.
Paul Yeah, well that was before.
Ian So you don't want to?
Paul Yeah.
Ian Doesn't bother me. Sit down will you.
Paul I'll be alright after I've, after...
Ian After what?
Paul Just after. It's easy for you, you've always known what you are, what you wanted, but I'm different.
Ian How?
Paul I like girls for a start.
Ian Do you?
Paul Doesn't bother you what people think does it.
Ian Not anymore, no.
Paul Can't do anything in this place, that's why I went to London.
Ian What did you do down there?

Paul Made a film.
Ian Come on. You'll like it, you know you will. You've liked it before.
Paul Fuck off will you and listen to me, you never bloody listen to me.
Ian Alright, I'm listening.
Paul No.
Ian Tell me.
Paul Stop telling us what to do.
Ian I'm not.
Paul You do.
Ian Sit down.
Paul I'll hit you.
Ian Do what?
Paul You heard.
Ian Sit down can't you.

Paul cuffs Ian over the head

You hit me.
Paul I said.
Ian Bloody mental you are.
Paul Yeah, runs in the family.
Ian How is your mam.
Paul I dunno.
Ian Doesn't anyone come round to see her?
Paul Like who.
Ian Doctor, social worker, you know.
Paul You used to be clever before you went to university.
Ian Is that why you're not stayin' at home, because of her?
Paul No. I got off at King's Cross and didn't know where the fuck I was, it was all just London—so I ended up working my way round the Monopoly board, asking for all the places I'd seen on telly. I was just like any other tourist, ended up in the West End. I had a toothbrush, bar of soap, pair of socks and a change of underwear. It was alright till the money run out.
Ian How long was that?
Paul About two days.
Ian Then what?
Paul I didn't have any money did I.
Ian Didn't you sign on?

Scene 18

Paul What d'you give as an address, the Embankment? Applied for a loan—to the Social like, for the deposit on a room—they wanted to know how I was gonna pay it back, so I said, "Instalments", the bloke laughed, he was alright, really.
Ian Where did you sleep?
Paul Anywhere—shop doorways, parks, squats, building sites, bridges, the Salvation Army give out sleeping bags. One night I went down Waterloo, the Bullring, a whole island sunk into the traffic, looks like summat out the Stone Age—bonfires, dogs, kids, smoke, drunks, people shouting, the old and the mad living in a cardboard box. And people just walk by, looking through you like you weren't there. One night were enough for me. I didn't sleep, always tired, always hungry, always soaked to the bone—one morning I got woke up with a hose pipe showering us down; they were cleaning the pavement, ready for people to walk on it. Anyroad... I was back at King's Cross one day... And this young fella comes up to us with a cup of tea...
Ian Yeah.
Paul Yeah—and he give us his tea.
Ian So.
Paul So I came home.
Ian I don't get it—why did he give you his tea?
Paul I dunno maybe he were a bit soft in the 'ead, I mean why else would someone give you summat for nowt. He invited me back to his place for the night. Nothing in it he says. It was a big house all the rooms empty but for one. He says to wait, so I sit on the bed—then this old man comes in puts a fiver down and takes off all his clothes. It was alright for a while—then one night I said "no" wanted to watch Laurel and Hardy on the telly instead—so they kicked us out. He was a grizzly ord bastard. I went down Piccadilly Circus and met up with some other lads; we had a good laugh. We hung round Soho mostly, in the pubs, picking up passing trade—old men married men young men the world without his wife. I only did it for the money. Had a couple of girlfriends—nothing serious like.
Ian What about your friend, the one you stay with.
Paul There isn't anyone.
Ian So who's your letter from then?
Paul I don't know, I haven't opened it yet.

Scene 19

The Gents in a night-club

Music is playing in the background

Billy is smoking

Steven enters

Steven Where's the party then?
Billy Dunno.
Steven Cheer up, it 'asnt 'appened yet.
Billy Just trying to cool down.
Steven What's up?
Billy Nothing.
Steven Why don't you just tell me to bog off? Get it eh? Bog off from a bog.
Billy Yeah, funny.
Steven Miserable sod. There's a funny smell in here.
Billy What smell? I can't smell anything.

Steven looks in the mirror

Steven If looks could kill I wouldn't be able to look in another mirror. (*He combs his hair*)
Billy Yeah, like the shirt.
Steven Frankie Boyds, got it half price in the fire sale—Nigel Squires tried to burn the place down after they gave him the sack.
Billy Yeah, I heard.
Steven Reet then, no point gabbin' in here all night is thee? I'm off to get caylied.
Billy Is Rosemary Tredwell still out there?
Steven God you stink.
Billy High Karate.
Steven That won't pull anything—what you need's one of these, (*he indicates the place on his trousers*) johnny pocket—sends out the message, ready, willing and prepared. What's that on your teeth?
Billy Where?

Scene 19

Steven There.
Billy I can't see anything.
Steven Open your mouth, wider.

Steven pops a Durex in Billy's mouth

Steven Chew on that, it'll give you something to think about.

Steven exits

In the night-club, Shirley and Mary are on the edge of the dance floor

Mary I feel so nervous.
Shirley Don't be, you look great.
Mary What if he says "no"?
Shirley He won't. Don't give him the chance, just grab him by the hand and get him on the dance floor.
Mary But when?
Shirley When you feel like it.
Mary I don't feel like it.
Shirley Then don't.
Mary Why are you always so negative?
Shirley What d'you mean, negative?
Mary The opposite of positive. You know what I mean.
Shirley No, I don't.
Mary If you think positively, that something's going to happen, then it will. But if you just stand about thinking negative thoughts, putting yourself down, thinking the worst all the time, then you can only expect the worst to happen.
Shirley Where d'you read that, back of a matchbox.
Mary It's true. You've got to be positive about life.
Shirley D'you want another drink?
Mary No.
Shirley No need to get like that.
Mary I'm not getting like anything.
Shirley Hang about.
Mary What?
Shirley So you're telling me, if I stand here and think that Phil Collins is gonna come through that door and ask me to marry him, he will?

Mary You don't like Phil Collins do you?
Shirley Yeah, why not?

Mary exits

Mary!

Paul is on the phone in the night-club

Paul Hello—hello—is anyone there? Can you hear me? I can't hear you—it's me, Paul—is anyone there?

Money runs out

Shit!

Ian is by himself in the night-club. He is writing in a little black notebook

Mary joins him

Mary Have you see Paul?
Ian What?
Mary Have you seen Paul?
Ian No.

Pause

Mary What's that you're writing?
Ian Nothing.
Mary Can I have a look?
Ian It's nothing.
Mary I write things in my head. Poems while I'm working. Would you like to hear one?
Ian Are they funny?
Mary No, should they be?
Ian No, I just thought they might be.
Mary Why?
Ian I don't know.
Mary You're not really interested are you?

Scene 19

Ian I am.
Mary Are you sure you haven't seen Paul?
Ian I said didn't I?
Mary No need to get shirty.
Ian I'm sorry, 1 was just——
Mary Why should they be funny?
Ian You don't understand.
Mary Don't I? You're a snob—write that in your little black notebook.

Mary exits

Paul Hello—hello—bloody answer me will you, I need you to answer me—bloody phone! (*He slams down the receiver*)

Ian joins Steven and Shirley who are sitting at a table on the edge of the dance floor

Steven Didn't expect to see you here tonight.
Ian I'm going tomorrow.
Steven I'll get you a drink.
Ian I've got an orange juice.
Steven What's up eh? On the penicillin? You hear that Shirley, the professor's on the wagon.
Shirley Silly cow.
Steven You what?
Shirley I said she's a silly cow.
Steven That's no way to talk about your mother, is it prof?
Shirley Mary, getting worked up over Paul.
Steven He's not worth it.
Ian That's why she's in a bad mood.
Shirley She's been looking for him all night.
Steven Funny that I haven't seen him since we got here—have you.
Shirley No. Please don't drink anymore.
Steven It's Saturday night, besides I've got something to celebrate.
Shirley What?
Steven I'll tell you later. So, back to university is it?
Ian Not straight off, no.
Shirley What you celebrating?
Steven Back to the bookworms.

Shirley Steven behave.
Steven I'm only joking, he knows that—don't you prof?
Ian Yeah.
Steven I wouldn't like it.
Shirley You can hardly read.
Steven Never judge a book by its cover. Bet you get some funny sorts there though, eh?
Ian Dead funny. There's some of the fellas, you can't tell what they are.
Steven What d'you mean?
Ian You know. Like if one came in here now and sat where I am, you wouldn't know—and before you knew it, he'd have his hand on your knee. (*He puts his hand on Steven's knee*)
Steven Get off.
Ian Straight up.
Steven Did you hear that?
Shirley Well you wouldn't have anything to worry about, you're ugly.
Steven Lot of foreigners, too.
Ian Yup.
Steven It's like this place, with all the Paki shops and Indians opening up. Don't get us wrong, I'm not prejudiced, I just want 'em to go home that's all.
Shirley Where to?
Steven Bradford. I wouldn't leave this place for all the tea in China—different for you though, you've got summat to go for—but Paul, he's just a drifter ain't he?
Shirley What's wrong with that?
Steven He's got no purpose.
Ian D'you want another pint?
Steven Aye.

He finishes the rest of his pint in one and gives his glass to Ian

The night is yet young.

The Gents

Billy is smoking

Nicky and Shirt enter

Scene 19

Nicky Lend us a fag mate.
Billy (*looking up*) It's me last one.
Nicky That's alright, we only want one.

He takes a cigarette from Billy

Don't we Shirt?
Shirt (*taking the cigarette from Nicky*) Yeah, so it's lucky we bumped into you like this.
Nicky Dead lucky.
Billy I was just off.

Nicky blocks Billy's exit

Nicky Where too, church?
Shirt You shouldn't take the piss out of God.
Billy I never did.
Nicky What's that you said about my sister?
Billy Nothin'—honest.

Nicky and Shirt exit with Billy

Paul is on the phone again

Paul Who's that?... I don't know you, who are you?... I want to speak to Jim... I can't... Because I'm not in London... it's long distance, I'm running out of money, it's urgent, I need him to... Shut up will you?... A club.. Tell him Paul rang, I'll ring him.

Steven, the worse for drink, is trying to pull Shirley on to the dance floor

Steven Come on Shirley.
Shirley I don't want to.
Steven You like it when we dance.
Shirley No.
Steven You'd prefer to dance with someone else?
Shirley Like who?
Steven What about Paul?
Shirley Don't be ridiculous.

Steven And you don't say anything else?
Shirley What else is there.
Steven Like well done Steven, congratulations.
Shirley You're drunk.
Steven So? I'm having a good time.
Shirley Well I'm not.
Steven Look—sh, sh—he said, "Steven, the job's yours", that's it—I'm in the betting business, I've got a trade.
Shirley Don't spit in my face.
Steven You stick with me girl, I'm gonna make a fuckin' fortune.
Shirley What does he want you to do this time, wash his car?
Steven You don't like it because he's my friend.
Shirley I don't trust him.
Steven It's favourites. Money for old rope, all you have to do is take their money—nobody wins.
Shirley I don't think Paul's coming back.
Steven Disappointed?
Shirley Why should I be?
Steven Listen, you'll like this—this fella comes in today, fifty quid like that, on the dogs—on the fucking dogs!
Shirley My glass is empty.
Steven One minute he had fifty quid and the next it was in the Bookie's pocket.
Shirley I liked it better when you wanted to be an engineer.
Steven He just gave it away, nobody forced him, nobody mugged him—fifty quid for two minutes' worth of dogs chasing round after a stuffed rabbit.

Paul and Ian

Paul Where's Billy?
Ian Where have you been?
Paul Where's Billy?
Ian He'll be alright. I'm going away tomorrow.
Paul Thanks.
Ian Come with me. We could go now, pack our bags and just leave—piss on this place together.
Paul Where's Billy?
Ian Come on.

Scene 19

Paul No.
Ian Why not?
Paul 'Cos I don't want to.
Ian Why?
Paul I'm off to look for Billy.

Steven and Shirley

Shirley There's Paul.
Steven Suppose you'd rather be talking to him.
Shirley No.
Steven You fancy him.
Shirley No, I don't.
Steven Yes, you do.
Shirley You're drunk.
Steven You fancy him.
Shirley Alright. I fancy him—satisfied?
Steven Yeah.

My Girl *by the Temptations plays. Mary pulls Paul on to the dance floor*

Paul I can't dance.
Mary What?
Paul I can't dance.
Mary Of course you can.
Paul I feel stupid.
Mary You don't look stupid. Just follow me, it's easy.

They dance. Steven comes up behind Paul, taps him on the shoulder, Paul turns his face and Steven punches it

Steven I'm gonna kill you.

Ian pulls Steven away from Paul

   The bastard slept with her, he slept with her.
Ian Stay over there!
Paul You want a fight?
Steven Yeah.

Paul Yeah?
Steven Yeah!
Ian (*moving between them*) Pack it in will you.
Paul I want to.
Steven I'm not scared of him.

Nicky and Shirt enter

Paul Outside, now!
Nicky What's goin' on here then?
Ian Fuck off Tredwell.
Steven I'm gonna kill the cunt.

Nicky and Shirt drag Ian out of the way. They all fight. When it becomes obvious that Paul has the upper hand on Steven, Nicky shoves Steven out of the way and pulls out his flick-knife on Paul

Paul Where's Billy?
Nicky Being cared for.

Shirt and Ian stop fighting. Shirt holds Ian back

Steven I didn't agree to knives.
Nicky He was beating the shit out of you.
Paul Why?
Nicky Because I don't like your pretty face.
Ian Kick him in the balls Steven.

Steven runs off

Shirt, unsure of what to do, slackens his grip on Ian, Ian pushes past him and rushes at Nicky. Nicky turns and slashes wildly with his knife

Nicky Get back!

Unintentionally, the knife slashes across Ian's stomach. He stands still

I said to keep back—I wasn't going to do anything, just scare him, I told you to keep back.

Scene 20

Shirt runs off

It was your own fault.
Paul Come on Nicky, do it.
Nicky He just came at me.
Paul I'm waiting.

Nicky exits.

Paul rips off his shirt, and uses it as a bandage round Ian's stomach

Scene 20

Ian and Paul

Ian Sit down will you.
Paul Watch it eh.
Ian Go outside if you want one.
Paul I don't want to go outside, I want a fag. If there's anywhere you need a fag it's hospital and they don't bloody let you.
Ian It was your idea we come here, I'm alright.
Paul We're stayin' till someone sees you.
Ian There's nothing wrong.
Paul You're bleeding, look at me shirt.
Ian I didn't ask you to wrap it round me—it just looks worse than it is that's all.
Paul What's taking them so long, I don't see what the hold-up is.
Ian Just have a fag will you.
Paul I can't. You'll need stitches.
Ian Give over, it's just a scratch.
Paul D'you fancy a drink?
Ian I'm still going away tomorrow—why don't you come with us?
Paul I've already said. Well, do you?
Ian What.
Paul Want a drink.
Ian No.
Paul You can't anyway, they might have to give you an anaesthetic.
Ian So why ask.

Paul 'Cos I'm looking after you.
Ian You have a drink if you want one.
Paul I don't.
Ian I'm not going back to college.
Paul You'll go back.
Ian I've decided.
Paul What you gonna do instead?
Ian I dunno.
Paul You'll go back.
Ian What are you gonna do? Who was that you were on the phone to?
Paul A friend, alright.
Ian In London—the one that you shagged.
Paul Who says I shagged anyone in London?
Ian Billy.
Paul Wish they'd hurry up and see you.
Ian Why won't you tell me?
Paul I've telled thee there's nothing to tell. She's older than me... She helped us out, said I could stay at her house for a while, so I did and we got a bit friendly. So she writes to me, I ring her up now and again, that's all there is.
Ian Why did you leave?
Paul Because I had to, to clear me 'ead and now you're doin' it in again.
Ian She married?
Paul I don't see what the hold-up is.
Ian Go home if you want.
Paul I don't.
Ian Have you fucked Shirley.
Paul What if I have, what's it to you.
Ian Nothing.
Paul I fuck who I like.
Ian Oh aye?
Paul Piss off.
Ian Whose girlfriend haven't you tried to fuck?
Paul You what.
Ian What about Rosemary Tredwell.
Paul I never touched her.
Ian You never learn do you, you can't just go round screwing everyone's girlfriend.
Paul Why not.

Ian Because you can't, you hear?
Paul Yeah, yeah.
Ian What's the matter with you eh, what's the matter.
Paul Nothing, alright.
Ian If you want a girlfriend get one.
Paul I don't.
Ian What do you want.
Paul You know don't you.
Ian What, what do I know.
Paul You've known all along.
Ian Known what?
Paul So why d'you want me to come away?
Ian I just think we could have a bit of fun, you know. You can always go to London after, maybe I'll come with you. I don't see what the problem is.
Paul Nothing, there's no problem—I'll think about it, alright, now stop goin' on.
Ian Have a fag.
Paul I can't.
Ian Go on.
Paul No.
Ian Have a fag.
Paul I'll go outside.

Scene 21

Billy's flat

Paul is filling a bag with his belongings. He tries to fit a pair of baseball shoes in, then leaves them out

Billy enters, arm in a sling

Billy Where are you going?
Paul London.
Billy I'm not coming then?
Paul No. You can come and visit when I get settled in.
Billy Yeah. D'you know where yet?

Paul No—wait till I get there.
Billy You won't have any problems though.
Paul Shouldn't think so. You'll be alright. How's the arm?
Billy You don't have to go you know—I don't mind sleeping on the couch all the time—it's more comfortable than the bed. There won't be any trains yet.
Paul I'm not takin' train.
Billy How you goin' then? I've got money.
Paul I don't want your money.

Billy hands Paul a five pound note

Billy Go on—for a cuppa tea like.
Paul I can't stay, I've got to go, right.
Billy It'll be alright for me to come and visit then.
Paul Yeah, I've already said 'aven't I—why don't you want to come anymore?
Billy No—if it doesn't work out you can always come back.
Paul Yeah.
Billy I'm on days next week.

Paul throws Billy the baseball boots

Paul A present—they won't fit in me bag.
Billy They're too big.
Paul Put some extra socks on then.
Billy Hang on—you've forgot summat.

Billy gives Paul a letter, opened

Paul Have you read it.
Billy Yeah.
Paul D'you read all my letters?
Billy No-just the ones from London, I steam them open. They're interesting.
Paul I don't open yours do I?
Billy I don't get any.
Paul You read it.
Billy An' if I did I wouldn't mind.

Paul You read it.
Billy That who you stay with in London is it?
Paul Yeah.
Billy You sure he won't mind me coming?
Paul Yeah.
Billy Sounds alright then.
Paul Yeah.
Billy It doesn't bother me you know.
Paul What doesn't bother you.
Billy I'm just saying—it doesn't bother me. How did you meet him.
Paul In a pub.
Billy That's nice.
Paul I didn't have any money.
Billy Buy you a drink did he.
Paul Yeah. We went back to his place and he didn't make me do anything we just slept in the same bed. It's like what he wants most is the company, like he just enjoys having me there. We have a laugh, he takes me places and I feel alright, he makes me feel alright. He never makes me do anything I don't want but I don't mind as long as we don't do it too often. I've told him I'm not queer says he knows says he understands. He always makes sure I'm alright—for money, you know.
Billy What's his name—I can never make out his signature.
Paul Jim.

They both laugh

Billy Why did you leave.
Paul I was beginning to like him.
Billy So why are you going back.
Paul I don't know that I am—wait and see what happens when I get there.

Scene 22

The café

Shirley Have you ever been to Eastbourne?
Mary No.
Shirley Me neither.

Mary Cold and dead like this place is it?
Shirley I don't know. Funny how it all just drops off isn't it—like there's no in-between, either there's people or there isn't.
Mary I hate the winter.
Shirley It's only September.
Mary It's cold.

Pause

Shirley I might be going to Eastbourne soon.
Mary When?
Shirley It's not definite—they're opening this new hotel and they want me down there on the desk.
Mary Is there no-one in Eastbourne they can get?
Shirley It's not definite. It's just they need someone with a bit of personality and life. I'd have me own room with *en suite* shower and bathroom.
Mary Don't need any chambermaids do they?
Shirley It's called The Wish Tower, four star.
Mary Some people have all the luck.
Shirley At least you've got a fella.
Mary So could you if you wanted.
Shirley Men aren't everything you know Mary.
Mary I know.

Pause

Where is Eastbourne?
Shirley Somewhere near London I think. Anyroad, it wouldn't be for long, six months at the most.
Mary Well I might not be here when you get back.
Shirley Where you going?
Mary I don't know.
Shirley I can always ring you.
Mary We're not married you know. (*She pauses*) Anything could happen in six months—I might enter a competition and win a ticket round the world, or I might just get on a plane and go far away to some exotic place.
Shirley Well if you do send us a postcard.

Steven and Nicky enter

Scene 22

That's it, I'm going.
Mary Sit down will you.
Steven Hello Shirley, how you keeping?
Shirley Fine.
Steven Haven't seen you for a while.
Shirley No, not since yesterday—I saw you following me.
Steven Anyone sitting there?
Shirley Yes.
Nicky Don't waste your breath, she's not worth the effort.
Mary Who let you out your cage?
Nicky G'ez a coffee Steve.
Shirley How much does he pay you?
Nicky And a cheese'n'onion butty while you're up there.

Steven exits

Nicky sits at another table

Shirley I can't go anywhere without him following me; even when I'm having a pee I keep expectin' him to poke his head round the door. Don't know why he's hanging round with Nicky Tredwell, thought he had more sense. And as for his hair it's just bloody daft, what's he want to go and stick all that glue on it for?
Mary Why don't you go and ask him?
Shirley I'm not interested.

Billy enters, arm out of sling

Mary Shirley's going to Eastbourne.
Billy Oh aye, what for?
Shirley It's not decided.

Steven enters with coffee and a sandwich

Shirley goes to leave and nearly bumps into Steven

Bloody hell Steven.

Shirley exits

Billy Got a card from Paul this morning. Sounds alright. Didn't say much mind, just hello.
Mary Is he still with that girl?
Billy Dunno, didn't say.
Steven Jesus, I haven't had a poke in weeks, if I don't have one soon I'll go barmy.
Nicky What d'you think your right hand's for?
Steven It's worn out. I keep getting these aches——
Nicky It's got mustard on it.
Steven Yeah, I like mustard.
Nicky I can't eat that—go and get us another.
Steven I haven't got any money.
Billy We could go to the pictures.
Mary There's nothing on.
Billy What about my place then? Get some cans in and watch the telly.

Shirley enters

Shirley Here, they're shutting this place down at the end of the week.
Mary Won't bother you will it, you'll be in Eastbourne—expect things stay open longer down there.
Billy And it's warmer.
Mary Shut up Billy.
Billy Well it is, it's nearer the Equator.
Nicky (*shouting*) How's the arm Billy?
Billy Yeah, great.
Mary Don't talk to him.
Nicky It's out the sling then.
Billy Yeah.
Mary God you're soft.
Shirley Don't say that—for any successful relationship to work, each partner must treat the other with mutual respect.
Mary I'm going out with him, not going into business with him.
Shirley That's why mine and Steven's relationship didn't work—I didn't respect him and all he could see me as was something to worship, a love goddess.
Mary Bloody hell, where d'you get that from?

Nicky comes over and offers his hand to Billy

Scene 22

Nicky No hard feelings like?
Billy I won't if you don't mind, it's still a bit sore.
Nicky Aye. We just got a bit carried away that's all. Nothing personal.
Billy Yeah.

Pause

Nicky Which one of them are you shagging then?
Shirley Both of us.
Mary Yeah both of us and at the same time.

Shirley and Mary exit

Billy I'd best be off. See you around then.
Nicky Expect so.
Billy Cheers Steve.
Steven Cheers.

Billy exits

What d'you go and ask a daft question like that for?
Nicky Felt like it.

Pause

Steven You don't think he is do you? I've never done it with two in a bed.
Nicky You can have me sandwich if you want.
Steven Yeah, ta.

Steven eats the sandwich. Nicky reads the paper. Silence

CURTAIN

FURNITURE AND PROPERTY LIST

Further dressing may be added at the director's discretion

Scene 1

On stage:　Ball
　　　　　　T-shirts
　　　　　　Postcard
　　　　　　Coin

Personal:　**Billy:** Coin

Scene 2

No props required

Scene 3

No props required

Scene 4

On stage:　Tables. *On one of them:* cup of coffee
　　　　　　Chairs

Personal:　**Ian:** sunglasses, newspaper
　　　　　　Nicky: packet of cigarettes
　　　　　　Billy: ball

Scene 5

Personal:　**Paul:** swimming trunks
　　　　　　Billy: letter

Scene 6

No props required

Scene 7

Off stage: Lolly and ice cream (**Paul**)

Personal: **Paul:** towel
Billy: towel

Scene 8

No props required

Scene 9

On stage: Cotton wool
Shaving mirror
Jeans
Letter
Shoes
Radio
Phone
Chair

Off stage: Water and cotton wool (**Billy**)

Scene 10

On stage: Boiling kettle
Envelope

Personal: **Paul:** envelope. *In it:* letter, ten pound note

Scene 11

No props required

Scene 12

On stage: As for Scene 10

Off stage: Glass (**Billy**)

Personal: **Paul:** matches

Scene 13

Personal: **Billy:** sweets (Blackjacks)

Scene 14

On stage: Same as Scene 4. Tables empty

Off stage: Bunch of flowers (**Shirt**)

Personal: **Paul:** cigarettes
Ian: coins

Scene 15

Off stage: Shoes (**Shirley**)

Scene 16

On stage: Same as Scene 4. On one table a doughnut on a plate

Off stage: Cappuccino (**Paul**)
2 bags of chips (**Ian**)

Scene 17

On stage: Pool cues
2 stools

Scene 18

On stage: Bottle of cider

Personal: **Paul:** lighter

Scene 19

Personal: **Billy:** cigarettes
Steven: comb, Durex, pint of lager
Ian: little black notebook, pen
Nicky: flick-knife

Scene 20

No props required

Scene 21

On stage: Bag
Baseball shoes

Personal: **Billy:** five pound note, letter

Scene 22

Off stage: Coffee, sandwich (**Steven**)

Personal: **Nicky:** newspaper

EFFECTS PLOT

Cue 1	After **Mary** exits *Ship's bell rings in the distance*	(Page 13)
Cue 2	**Billy** tries to steam open a letter *Door bell rings, then again, long and insistent*	(Page 25)
Cue 3	**Paul** turns on the radio *Pop music*	(Page 28)
Cue 4	**Paul**: "I'm not at that number anymore——" *Loud slam of a door*	(Page 28)
Cue 5	**Billy**: "I'll get a glass of water, then." *Phone rings continuously*	(Page 29)
Cue 6	As Scene 19 opens *Music in the background*	(Page 56)
Cue 7	**Steven**: "Yeah." *Music:* My Girl *by the Temptations*	(Page 63)

www.ingramcontent.com/pod-product-compliance
Ingram Content Group UK Ltd.
Pitfield, Milton Keynes, MK11 3LW, UK
UKHW021844210426
5322IPUK00022B/465